Microsoft Publisher 2016 Keyboard Shortcuts

For Windows

By

U. C-Abel Books.

All Rights Reserved

Table of Contents

Acknowledgement.

U. C-Abel Books will not take all the credits for Microsoft Publisher 2016 keyboard shortcuts listed in this book, but shares it with Microsoft Corporation because some of the shortcut keys came from them and are "used with permission from Microsoft".

Dedication

This book is dedicated to computer users and lovers of keyboard shortcuts all over the world.

Introduction.

We enjoy using shortcut keys because they set us on a high plane that astonishes people around us when we work with them. As wonderful shortcuts users, the worst eyesore we witness in computing is to see somebody sluggishly struggling to execute a task through mouse usage when in actual sense shortcuts will help to save that person the time wasted. Most people have asked us to help them with a list of shortcut keys that can make them work as smartly as we do and that drove us into research to broaden our knowledge and truly help them as they demanded, that is the reason for the existence of this book. It is a great tool for lovers of shortcuts, and those who want to join the group.

Most times, the things we love don't come by easily. It is our love for keyboard shortcuts that made us to bear long sleepless nights like owls, just to make sure we get the best out of it, and it is the best we got that we are sharing with you in this book. You cannot be the same at computing after reading this book. The time you entrusted to our care is an expensive possession and we promise not to mess it up.

Thank you.

What to Know Before You Begin.

General Notes.

1. It is important to note that when using shortcuts to perform any command, you should make sure the target area is active, if not, you may get a wrong result. Example, if you want to highlight all texts, you must make sure the text field is active and if an object, make sure the object area is active. The active area is always known by the location where the cursor of your computer blinks.

2. Most of the keyboard shortcuts you will see in this book refer to the U.S. keyboard layout. Keys for other layouts might not correspond exactly to the keys on a U.S. keyboard.

3. The plus (+) signs that come in the middle of keyboard shortcuts simply mean the keys are meant to be combined or held down together not to be added as one of the shortcut keys. In a case where plus sign is needed; it will be duplicated (++).

4. For keyboard shortcuts in which you press one key immediately followed by another key, the keys are separated by a comma (,).

5. It is also important to note that the shortcut keys listed in this book are for Microsoft Publisher 2016.

Short Forms Used in This Book and Their Full Meaning.

The following are short forms of keyboard shortcuts used in this Microsoft Publisher 2016 Shortcuts book and their full meaning.

1.	Alt	-	Alternate Key
2.	Caps Lock	-	Caps Lock Key
3.	Ctrl	-	Control Key
4.	Esc	-	Escape Key
5.	F	-	Function Key
6.	Num Lock	-	Number Lock Key
7.	Shft	-	Shift Key
8.	Tab	-	Tabulate Key
9.	Win	-	Windows logo key
10.	Prt sc	-	Print Screen

CHAPTER 1.

Gathering The Basic Knowledge Of Keyboard Shortcuts.

Without the existence of the keyboard, there wouldn't have been anything like keyboard shortcuts, so in this chapter we will learn a little about keyboard before moving to keyboard shortcuts.

1. Definition of Computer Keyboard.
This is an input device that is used to send data to the computer memory.

Sketch of a Keyboard

1.1 Types of Keyboard.

   i. Standard (Basic) Keyboard.
   ii. Enhanced (Extended) Keyboard.

i. **Standard Keyboard:** This is a keyboard designed during the 1800s for mechanical typewriters with just 10 function keys (F keys) placed at the left side of it.

ii. **Enhanced Keyboard:** This is the current 101 to 102-key keyboard that is included in almost all the personal computers (PCs) of nowadays, which has 12 function keys at the top side of it.

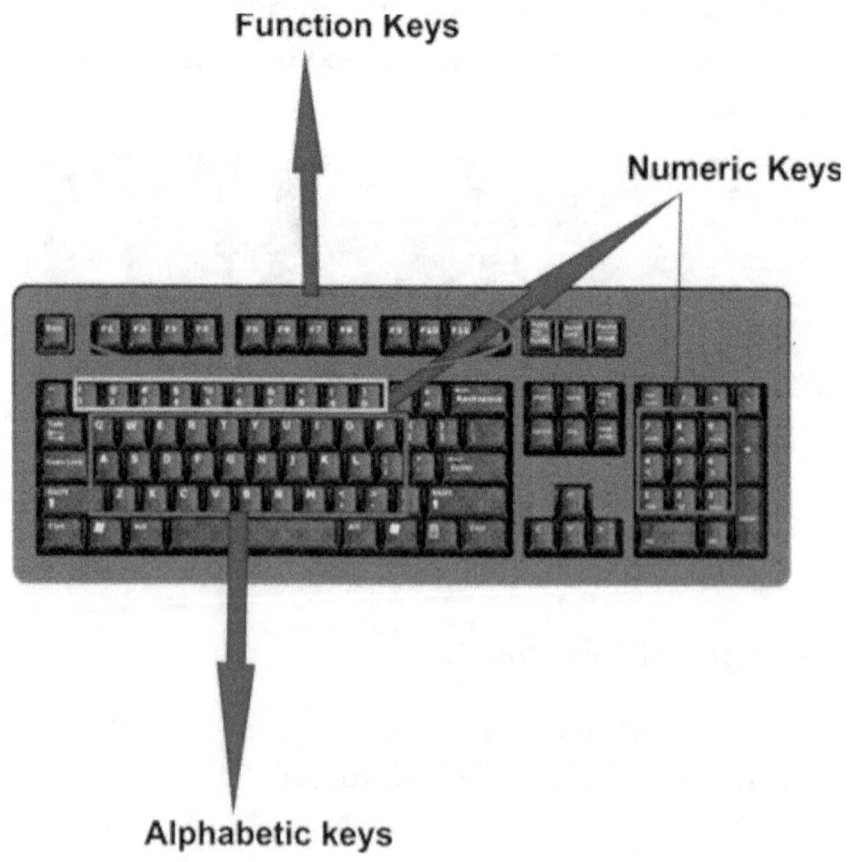

Function Keys

Numeric Keys

Alphabetic keys

1.2 Segments of the keyboard

- Numeric keys
- Alphabetic keys
- Punctuation keys
- Windows Logo key.
- Function keys
- Special keys

Numeric Keys: Numeric keys are keys with numbers from **0 - 9**.

Alphabetic Keys: These are keys that have alphabets on them, ranging from **A-Z**.

Punctuation Keys: These are keys of the keyboard used for punctuation. Examples include comma, full stop, colon, question marks, hyphen etc.

Windows Logo Key: A key on Microsoft Computer keyboard with its logo displayed on it. Search for this ⊞ on your keyboard.

Function Keys: These are keys that have **F** on them which are usually combined with other keys. They are F1 - F12, and are also in the class called Special Keys.

Special Keys: These are keys that perform special functions. They include: Tab, Ctrl, Caps lock, Insert,

Prt sc, alt gr, Shift, Home, Num lock, Esc and many others. Special keys work according to the type of computer involved. In some keyboard layout, especially laptops, the keys that turn the speaker on/off, the one that increases/decreases volume, the key that turns the computer Wifi on/off are also special keys.

Other Special Keys Worthy of Note.

Enter Key: This is located at the right-hand corner of the keyboard. It is used to send messages to the computer to execute commands, in most cases it is used to mean "Ok" or "Go".

Escape Key (ESC): This is the first key on the upper left of the keyboard. It is used to cancel routines, close menus and select options such as **Save** according to circumstance.

Control Key (CTRL): It is located on the bottom row of the left and right hand side of the keyboard. They also work with the function keys to execute commands using Keyboard shortcuts (key combinations).

Alternate Key (ALT): It is located on the bottom row, very close to the CTRL key on both side of the keyboard. It enables many editing functions to be accomplished by using some keystroke combinations on the keyboard.

Shift Key: This adds to the functions of the function keys. In addition, it enables the use of alternative function of a particular button (key), especially, those with more than one function on a key. E.g. use of capital letters, symbols and numbers.

1.3. Selecting/Highlighting With the Keyboard.

This is a highlighting method or style where data is selected using the keyboard instead of a computer mouse.

To do this:

- Move your cursor to the text you want to highlight, make sure that area is active,
- Hold down the shift key with one finger
- Then use another finger to move the arrow key that points to the direction you want to highlight.

1.4 The Operating Modes Of The Keyboard.

Just like the mouse the keyboard has two operating modes. The two modes are Text Entering and Command Mode.

a. **Text Entering Mode:** this mode gives the operator/user the opportunity to type text.

b.   **Command Mode:** this is used to command the operating system/software/application to execute commands in certain ways.

2. Ways To Improve In Your Typing Skill.

1. Put Your Eyes Off The Keyboard.

This is the aspect of keyboard usage that many don't find funny because they always ask. "How can I put my eyes off the keyboard when I am running away from the occurrence of errors on my file?" My aim is to be fast, is this not going to slow me down?

Of course, there will be errors and at the same time your speed will slow down but the motive behind the introduction of this method is to make you faster than you are. Looking at your keyboard while you type can make you get a sore neck, it is better you learn to touch type because the more you type with your eyes fixed on the screen instead of the keyboard, the faster you become.

An alternative to keeping your eyes off your keyboard is to use the *"Das Keyboard Ultimate"*.

2. Errors Challenge You

It is better to fail than not to try at all. Not trying at all is an attribute of the weak and lazybones. When you make mistakes, try again because errors are opportunities for improvement.

3. Good Posture (Position Yourself Well).
Do not adopt an awkward position while typing. You should get everything on your desk organized or arranged before sitting to type. Your posture while typing contributes to your speed and productivity.

4. Practice
Here is the conclusion of everything said above. You have to practice your shortcuts constantly. The practice alone is a way of improvement. "Practice brings improvement". Practice always.

2.1 Software That Will Help You Improve In Your Typing Skill.

There are several Software programs for typing that both kids and adults can use for their typing skill. Here is a list of software that can help you improve in your typing: Mavis Beacon, Typing Instructor, Mucky Typing Adventure, Rapid Tying Tutor, Letter Chase Tying Tutor, Alice Touch Typing Tutor and many more. Personally, I recommend Mavis Beacon.

To learn typing with MAVIS BEACON, install Mavis Beacon software to your computer, start with keyboard lesson, then move to games. Games like **Penguin Crossing, Creature Lab** or **Space Junk** will help you become a professional in typing. Typing and keyboard shortcuts work hand-in-hand.

Sketch of a computer mouse

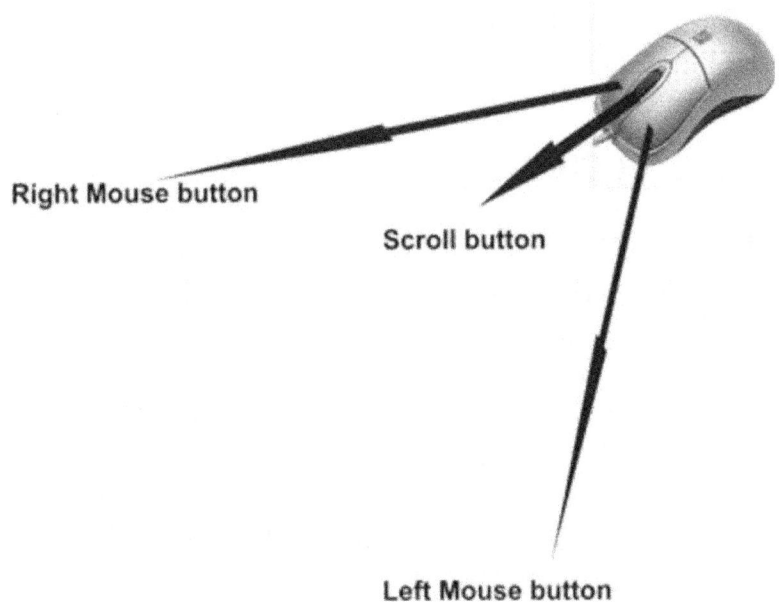

Right Mouse button

Scroll button

Left Mouse button

3. Mouse:

This is an oval-shaped portable input device with three buttons for scrolling, left clicking, and right clicking that enables work to be done effectively on a computer. The plural form of mouse is mice.

3.1 Types of Computer Mouse

- Mechanical Mouse
- Optical Mechanical Mouse (Optomechanical)
- Laser Mouse
- Optical Mouse

- BlueTrack Mouse

3.2 Forms of Clicking:

Left Clicking: This is the process of clicking the left side button of the mouse. It can be called *clicking* without the addition of *left*.

Right Clicking: It is the process of clicking the right side button of the mouse.

Double Clicking: It is the process of clicking the left side button two times (twice) and immediately.

Double clicking is used to select a word while thrice clicking is used to select a sentence or paragraph.

Scroll Button: It is the little key attached to the mouse that looks like a tiny wheel. It takes you up and down a page when moved.

3.3 Mouse Pad: This is a small soft mat that is placed under the mouse to make it have a free movement.

3.4 Laptop Mouse Touchpad

This unlike the mouse we explained above is not external, rather it is inbuilt (comes with a laptop computer). With the presence of a laptop mouse touchpad, an external mouse is not needed to use a laptop, except in a case where it is malfunctioning or the operator prefers to use external one for some reasons.

The laptop mouse touchpad is usually positioned at the end of the keyboard section of a laptop computer. It is rectangular in shape with two buttons positioned below it. The two buttons/keys are used for left and right clicking just like the external mouse. Some laptops come with four mouse keys. Two placed above the mouse for left and right clicking and two other keys placed below it for the same function.

4. Definition Of Keyboard Shortcuts.

Keyboard shortcuts are defined as a series of keys, sometimes with combination that execute tasks that typically involve the use of mouse or other input devices.

5. Why You Should Use Shortcuts.

1. One may not be able to use a computer mouse easily because of disability or pain.

2. One may not be able to see the mouse pointer as a result of vision impairment, in such case what will the person do? The answer is SHORTCUT.

3. Research has made it known that Extensive mouse usage is related to Repetitive Syndrome Injury (RSI) greatly than the use of keyboard.

4. Keyboard shortcuts speed up computer users, making learning them a worthwhile effort.

5. When performing a job that requires precision, it is wise that you use the keyboard instead of mouse, for instance, if you are dealing with Text Editing, it is better you handle it using keyboard shortcuts than spending more time with mouse alone.

6. Studies calculate that using keyboard shortcuts allows working 10 times faster than working with the mouse. The time you spend looking for the mouse and then getting the cursor to the position you want is lost! Reducing your work duration by 10 times brings you greater results.

5.1 Ways To Become A Lover Of Shortcuts.

1. Always have the urge to learn new shortcut keys associated with the programs you use.
2. Be happy whenever you learn a new shortcut.
3. Try as much as you can to apply the new shortcuts you learnt.
4. Always bear it in mind that learning new shortcuts is worth it.

5. Always remember that the use of keyboard shortcuts keeps people healthy while performing computing activities.

5.2 How To Learn New Shortcut Keys

1. Do a research for them: quick reference (a cheat sheet comprehensively compiled) can go a long way to help you improve.
2. Buy applications that show you keyboard shortcuts every time you execute an action with the mouse.
3. Disconnect your mouse if you must learn this fast.
4. Read user manuals and help topics (Whether offline or online).

5.3 Your Reward For Knowing Shortcut Keys.

1. You will get faster unimaginably.
2. Your level of efficiency will increase.
3. You will find it easy to use.
4. Opportunities are high that you will become an expert in what you do.
5. You won't have to go for **Office button**, click **New,** click **Blank and Recent** and click **Create** just to insert a fresh/blank page. **Ctrl +N** takes care of that in a second.

A Funny Note: Keyboard Shortcuts and Mousing are in a marital union with Keyboard Shortcuts being the head and it will be unfair for anybody to put asunder between them.

5.4 Why We Emphasize On The Use of Shortcuts.

You may never ditch your mouse completely unless you are ready to make your brain a box of keyboard shortcuts which will really be frustrating. Just imagine yourself learning all the shortcuts for the programs you use and its various versions. You shouldn't learn keyboard shortcuts that way.

Why we are emphasizing on the use of shortcuts is because mouse usage is becoming unusually common and unhealthy, too. So we just want to make sure both are combined so you can get fast, productive and healthy in your computing activities. All you need to know is just the most important ones associated with the programs you use.

CHAPTER 2.

15 (Fifteen) Special Keyboard Shortcuts.

The fifteen special keyboard shortcuts are fifteen (15) shortcut keys every computer user should know.

The following table contains the list of keyboard shortcuts every computer user should know.

1.   **Ctrl + A:** Control plus A, highlights or selects everything you have in the environment where you are working.

> *If you are like **"Wow, the content of this document is large and there is no time to select all of it, besides, it's going to mount pressure on my computer?"** Using the mouse for this is an outdated method of handling a task like selecting all, Ctrl+A will take care of that within seconds.*

2.   **Ctrl + C:** Control plus C copies any highlighted or selected element within the work environment.

> *Saves the time and stress which would have been used to right click and click again just to copy. Use ctrl+c.*

3. **Ctrl + N:** Control plus N opens a new window.

    Instead of clicking **File, New, blank/ template** *and another* **click***, just press* **Ctrl + N** *and a fresh window will appear instantly.*

4. **Ctrl + O:** Control plus O opens a new program.

    Use ctrl +O when you want to locate or open a file or program.

5. **Ctrl + P:** Control plus P prints the active document.

    Always use this to locate the printer dialog box and print.

6. **Ctrl + S:** Control plus S saves a new document or file and changes made by the user.

    Going for the mouse? Please stop! Don't use the mouse. Just press Ctrl+S and everything will be saved.

7. **Ctrl +V:** Control plus V pastes copied elements into the active area of the program in use.

    Using ctrl+V in a case like this Saves the time and stress of right clicking and clicking again just to paste.

8. **Ctrl + W:** Control plus W is used to close the page you are working on when you want to leave the work environment.

> ***"There is a way Peace does this without using the mouse. Oh my God, why didn't I learn it then?"*** Don't worry, I have the answer, Peace presses Ctrl+W to close active windows.

9. **Ctrl + X:** Control plus X cuts elements (making the elements to disappear from their original place). The difference between cutting and deleting elements is that in Cutting, what was cut doesn't get lost permanently but prepares itself so that it can be pasted in another location selected by the user.

> *Use ctrl+x when you think* ***"this shouldn't be here and I can't stand the stress of retyping or redesigning it in the rightful place it belongs".***

10. **Ctrl + Y:** Control plus Y redoes an undone action.

> *Ctrl+Z brought back what you didn't need? Press Ctrl+ Y to remove it again.*

11. **Ctrl + Z:** Control plus Z undoes actions.

Can't find what you typed now or a picture you inserted, it suddenly disappeared or you mistakenly removed it? Press Ctrl+Z to bring it back.

12. **Alt + F4:** Alternative plus F4 closes active windows or items.

   *You don't need to move the mouse in order to close an active window, just press **Alt + F4** if you are done or don't want somebody who is coming to see what you are doing.*

13. **Ctrl + F6:** Control plus F6 Navigates between open windows, making it possible for a user to see what is happening in windows that are active.
   Are you working in Microsoft Word and want to find out if the other active window where your browser is loading a page is still progressing? Use Ctrl + F6.

14. **F1:** This displays the help window.

   *Is your computer malfunctioning? Use **F1** to find help when you don't know what next to do.*

15. **F12:** This enables user to make changes to an already saved document.
   F12 is the shortcut to use when you want to change the format in which you saved your existing document, password it, change its

name, change the file location or destination, or make other changes to it. It will save your time.

CHAPTER 3.

Keyboard Shortcuts In Publisher 2016.

Definition of Program: Microsoft Publisher is a program designed by Microsoft in 1991 for Desktop Publishing. It is included in Office 2016 bundle.

The following list contains keyboard shortcuts that will boost your productivity in Microsoft Publisher.

Ribbon Shortcuts.

These shortcuts were introduced with the Publisher ribbon. Some tabs are contextual and appear only when you've inserted or selected an object such as a shape or a table. The double-letter shortcuts make it possible to use keyboard shortcuts with contextual tabs.

To use these, first selected the object, then press Alt, press the two letter context menu shortcut, and then press the remaining keys if any. For example to open the **Shape Effects** menu and add a shadow to a shape you select the shape, press **Alt**, **JD** to open the **Drawing Tools – Format** tab, **SE** to open the **Shape Effects** menu, **S** to select the **Shadow Gallery**, and then tab through the shadow options to apply the shadow to your shape.

Shape and Picture Effects

Shape Effects

TASK	SHORTCUT
Open the **Shape Effects Menu**	Alt, JD, SE
Open the **Shape Effects – Shadow Gallery**	Alt, JD, SE, S - then tab through options
Open the **Shape Effects – Reflection Gallery**	Alt, JD, SE, R - then tab through options
Open the **Shape Effects – Glow Gallery**	Alt, JD,SE,G- then tab through options
Open the **Shape Effects – Soft Edges Gallery**	Alt, JD,SE,E - then tab through options
Open the **Shape Effects – Bevel Gallery**	Alt, JD,SE,B - then tab through options
Open the **Shape Effects – 3-D Rotation Gallery**	Alt, JD,SE,D - then tab through options
Open the **Shape Styles Gallery**	Alt, JD,ST - then tab through options

Picture effects

TASK	SHORTCUT
Open the **Picture Effects Menu**	Alt, JP,PE
Open the **Picture Effects – Shadow Gallery**	Alt, JP,PE,S - then tab through options
Open the **Picture Effects – Reflection Gallery**	Alt, JP,PE,R - then tab through options
Open the **Picture Effects – Glow Gallery**	Alt, JP,PE,G - then tab through options

21

Open the **Picture Effects – Soft Edges Gallery**	Alt, JP,PE,E - then tab through options
Open the **Picture Effects – Bevel Gallery**	Alt, JP,PE,B - then tab through options
Open the **Picture Effects – 3-D Rotation Gallery**	Alt, JP,PE,D - then tab through options
Open the **Picture Styles Gallery**	Alt, JP,K - then tab through options
Clear **Picture Style**	Alt, JP,K,C

Text Effects

Text fill dropdown

TASK	SHORTCUT
Open Text Fill Dropdown	Alt, JX,TI
No Fill	Alt, JX,TI,N - then tab through options
More Fill Colors...	Alt, JX,TI,M - then tab through options
Fill Effects...	Alt, JX,TI,F - then tab through options
Tints	Alt, JX,TI,T - then tab through options
Sample Font Color	Alt, JX,TI,S

Text outline dropdown

TASK	SHORTCUT
Open Text Outline Dropdown	Alt ,JX,TO
No Outline	Alt ,JX,TO,N

More Outline Colors...	Alt, JX,TO,M - then tab through options
Outline Effects...	Alt. JX.TO.O - then tab through options
Sample Line Color	Alt, JX,TO,S - then tab through options
Weight	Alt, JX,TO,W - then tab through options
Dashes	Alt, JX,TO,D - then tab through options

Text effects dropdown

TASK	SHORTCUT
Open Text Effects Dropdown	Alt, JX,TE
Shadow	Alt, JX, TE,S - then tab through options
Reflection	Alt, JX, TE,R - then tab through options
Glow	Alt, JX, TE,G - then tab through options
Bevel	Alt, JX, TE,B - then tab through options

Create, Open, Close, Or Save A Publication

Create, open, close a publication

TASK	SHORTCUT
Open a new instance of Publisher	CTRL+N

Display the **Open Publication** dialog box	CTRL+O
Close the current publication	CTRL+F4 or CTRL+W
Display the **Save As** dialog box	CTRL+S

Edit Or Format Text Or Objects

Edit or format text

TASK	SHORTCUT
Display the **Find and Replace** task pane, with the **Find** option selected	F3 or CTRL+F or SHIFT+F4
Display the **Find and Replace** task pane, with the **Replace** option selected	CTRL+H
Check spelling	F7
Display the **Thesaurus** task pane	SHIFT+F7
Display the **Research** task pane	ALT + click a word
Select all the text (If the cursor is in a text box, this selects all text in the current story; if the cursor is not in a text box, this selects all the objects on a page.)	CTRL+A
Make text bold	CTRL+B
Italicize text	CTRL+I
Underline text	CTRL+U
Make text small capital letters,	CTRL+SHIFT+K

or return small capital letters to upper and lower case	
Open the **Font** dialog	CTRL+SHIFT+F
Copy formatting	CTRL+SHIFT+C
Paste formatting	CTRL+SHIFT+V
Turn **Special Characters** on or off	CTRL+SHIFT+Y
Return character formatting to the current text style	CTRL+SPACEBAR
Apply or remove subscript formatting	CTRL+=
Apply or remove superscript formatting	CTRL+SHIFT+=
Increase space between letters in a word (kerning)	CTRL+SHIFT+]
Decrease space between letters in a word (kerning)	CTRL+SHIFT+[
Increase font size by 1.0 point	CTRL+]
Decrease font size by 1.0 point	CTRL+[
Increase to the next size in the **Font Size** box	CTRL+SHIFT+>
Decrease to the next size in the **Font Size** box	CTRL+SHIFT+<
Center a paragraph	CTRL+E
Align a paragraph on the left	CTRL+L
Align a paragraph on the right	CTRL+R
Align a paragraph on both sides (justified)	CTRL+J
Distribute a paragraph evenly horizontally	CTRL+SHIFT+D
Set newspaper alignment for a paragraph (East Asian	CTRL+SHIFT+J

languages only)	
Display the **Hyphenation** dialog box	CTRL+SHIFT+H
Insert the current time	ALT+SHIFT+T
Insert the current date	ALT+SHIFT+D
Insert the current page number	ALT+SHIFT+P
Prevent the word from getting hyphenated if it occurs at the end of a line	CTRL+SHIFT+0 (zero)

Copy text formats

TASK	SHORTCUT
Copy formatting from the selected text	CTRL+SHIFT+C
Apply copied formatting to text	CTRL+SHIFT+V

Copy, cut, paste or delete text or objects

TASK	SHORTCUT
Copy the selected text or object	CTRL+C or CTRL+INSERT
Cut the selected text or object	CTRL+X or SHIFT+DELETE
Paste text or an object	CTRL+V or SHIFT+INSERT
Delete the selected object	DELETE or CTRL+SHIFT+X

Undo or redo an action

TASK	SHORTCUT

Undo what you last did	CTRL+Z or ALT+BACKSPACE
Redo what you last did	CTRL+Y or F4

Nudge an object

TASK	SHORTCUT
Nudge a selected object up, down, left, or right	Arrow keys
If the selected object has a cursor in its text, nudge the selected object up, down, left, or right	ALT+arrow keys

Layer Objects

TASK	SHORTCUT
Bring object to front	ALT+F6
Send object to back	ALT+SHIFT+F6

Snap Objects

TASK	SHORTCUT
Turn **Snap to Guides** on or off	F10, SHIFT+R, SHIFT+S, SHIFT+M

Select or Group Objects

TASK	SHORTCUT
Select all objects on the page (If your cursor is in a text box, this selects all the text in a story)	CTRL+A
Group selected objects, or	CTRL+SHIFT+G

ungroup grouped objects	
Clear the selection from selected text	ESC
Clear the selection from a selected object	ESC
Select the object within the group — if that object contains selected text	ESC

Work With Pages.

Select or insert pages

If your publication is in Two-Page Spread view, these commands apply to the selected two-page spread. Otherwise, these apply only to the selected page.

TASK	SHORTCUT
Display the **Go To Page** dialog box	F5 or CTRL+G
Insert a page or a two-page spread. If you are creating a newsletter, it opens the **Insert publication type Pages** dialog box	CTRL+SHIFT+N
Insert duplicate page after the selected page	CTRL+SHIFT+U

Move between pages

TASK	SHORTCUT
Display the **Go To Page** dialog box.	F5 or CTRL+G

Go to the next page	CTRL+PAGE DOWN
Go to the previous page	CTRL+PAGE UP
Switch between the current page and the master page	CTRL+M

Use the master page

TASK	SHORTCUT
Switch between the current page and the master page.	CTRL+M

Show or hide boundaries or guides

TASK	SHORTCUT
Turn **Boundaries** on or off.	CTRL+SHIFT+O
Turn **Horizontal Baseline Guides** on or off (not available in web view)	CTRL+F7
Turn **Vertical Baseline Guides** on or off (East Asian languages only—not available in web view)	CTRL+SHIFT+F7

Zoom

TASK	SHORTCUT
Switch between the current view and the actual size	F9
Zoom to full page view	CTRL+SHIFT+L

Printing

Using Print Preview

These keyboard shortcuts are available when you're in **Print** view and affect the print preview pane.

TASK	SHORTCUT
Switch between the current view and the actual size	F9
Scroll up or down	UP ARROW or DOWN ARROW
Scroll left or right	LEFT ARROW or RIGHT ARROW
Scroll up in large increments	PAGE UP or CTRL+UP ARROW
Scroll down in large increments	PAGE DOWN or CTRL+DOWN ARROW
Scroll left in large increments	CTRL+LEFT ARROW
Scroll right in large increments	CTRL+RIGHT ARROW
Scroll to the upper left corner of the page	HOME
Scroll to the lower right corner of the page	END
Display the **Go To Page** dialog box	F5 or CTRL+G
Go to the previous page	CTRL+PAGE UP
Go to the next page	CTRL+PAGE DOWN
Go to the next window (if you have multiple publications open)	CTRL+F6
Exit **Print Preview** and	CTRL+P

display the **Print** view	
Exit **Print Preview**	ESC

Print a publication

TASK	SHORTCUT
Open the **Print** dialog view.	CTRL+P

Work With Web Pages and Email

Insert hyperlinks

TASK	SHORTCUT
Display the **Insert Hyperlink** dialog box (make sure your cursor is in a text box)	CTRL+K

Send e-mail

After you choose **Send as Message** (**File** > **Share** > **Email**), you can use the following keyboard shortcuts.

Important: Outlook needs to be open before you can send email messages. If Outlook isn't open, the message will be stored in your **Outbox** folder.

TASK	SHORTCUT
Send the current page or publication	ALT+S
Open the **Address Book** (cursor must be in the message header)	CTRL+SHIFT+B

Open the **Design Checker** (cursor must be in the message header)	ALT+K
Check the names on the **To, Cc,** and **Bcc** lines (cursor must be in the message header)	CTRL+K
Open the **Address Book** with the **To** box selected (cursor must be in the message header)	ALT+. (period)
Open the **Address Book** with the **Cc** box selected (cursor must be in the message header)	ALT+C
Open the **Address Book** with the **Bcc** box selected (cursor must be in the message header and the **Bcc** field must be visible)	ALT+B
Go to the **Subject** box	ALT+J
Open the Outlook **Message Options** dialog box	ALT+P
Open the **Custom** dialog box to create an email message flag (cursor must be in the email message header)	CTRL+SHIFT+G
Move the cursor to the next field in the email message header (cursor must be in the email message header)	TAB
Move the cursor to the previous field in the email message header	SHIFT+TAB
Alternate between the insertion point in the email message header and the **Send** button in	CTRL+TAB

the **Mailing** toolbar	
Open the **Address Book** when the cursor is in the e-mail message header	CTRL+SHIFT+B

Automate Tasks

Work with macros

TASK	SHORTCUT
Display the **Macros** dialog box.	ALT+F8

Work with Visual Basic

TASK	SHORTCUT
Display the Visual Basic editor	ALT+F11

Customer's Page.

This page is for customers who enjoyed Microsoft Publisher 2016 Keyboard Shortcuts For Windows.

Dearly beloved customer, please leave a review behind if you enjoyed this book or found it helpful. It will be highly appreciated, thank you.

Other Books By This Publisher.

S/N	Title	Series
Series A: Limits Breaking Quotes.		
1	Discover Your Key Christian Quotes	Limits Breaking Quotes
Series B: Shortcut Matters.		
1	Windows 7 Shortcuts	Shortcut Matters
2	Windows 7 Shortcuts & Tips	Shortcut Matters
3	Windows 8.1 Shortcuts	Shortcut Matters
4	Windows 10 Shortcut Keys	Shortcut Matters
5	Microsoft Office 2007 Keyboard Shortcuts For Windows.	Shortcut Matters
6	Microsoft Office 2010 Shortcuts For Windows.	Shortcut Matters
7	Microsoft Office 2013 Shortcuts For Windows.	Shortcut Matters
Series C: Teach Yourself.		
1	Teach Yourself Computer Fundamentals	Teach Yourself
Series D: For Painless Publishing		
1	Self-Publish it with CreateSpace.	For Painless Publishing
2	Where is my money? Now solved for Kindle and CreateSpace	For Painless Publishing
3	Describe it on Amazon	For Painless Publishing
4	How To Market That Book.	For Painless Publishing